Komodo Dragons

LIFE CYCLES

Tracey Reeder

PICTURE CREDITS

Cover: photograph of a Komodo dragon in Indonesia © Martin Harvey/Corbis/Tranz.

Photographs; page 1 © W. Perry Conway/Corbis/Tranz; page 4 (bottom left) © Keren Su/Corbis/Tranz; page 4 (bottom right), Photodisc; page 5 (top) © Stephen Frink/Corbis/Tranz; page 5 (bottom left), Photodisc; page 5 (bottom right), Photodisc; page 6 © Stock Image Group/SPL; page 8 © Bool Dan/Corbis/Tranz; page 9 © Natalie Fobes/Corbis/Tranz; page 12, photograph of a Komodo hatching from an egg, courtesy of Duane Meier; page 13 © Wolfgang Kaehler/Corbis/Tranz; page 14 © W. Perry Conway/Corbis/Tranz; page 15 © Michael K Nichols/National Geographic/Getty Images; page 16 © Bool Dan/Corbis/Tranz; page 21 © Melina Mara/TheSUN, Bremerton, WA; page 22 (bottom left) © images.com/Corbis/Tranz; page 22 (bottom right) © Charles & Josette Lenars /Corbis/Tranz; page 23, photograph of Point Defiance Zoo in Tacoma, courtesy of Sue Vernon/Point Defiance Zoo & Aquarium; page 25, photograph of a Komodo dragon in Honolulu Zoo, courtesy of Duane Meier; page 26 © Wolfgang Kaehler/Corbis/Tranz; page 29, Corbis.

Illustrations on pages 11 and 19 by Elena Petrov and Jamie Laurie.

Special thanks to Caroline Allen for use of her article on the Seattle Post-Intelligencer website (http://seattlepi.nwsource.com/lifestyle/drag14.shtml).

Produced through the worldwide resources of the National Geographic Society, John M. Fahey, Jr., President and Chief Executive Officer; Gilbert M. Grosvenor, Chairman of the Board; Nina D. Hoffman, Executive Vice President and President, Books and Education Publishing Group.

PREPARED BY NATIONAL GEOGRAPHIC SCHOOL PUBLISHING
Ericka Markman, Senior Vice President and President, Children's Books and Education Publishing Group; Steve Mico, Vice President and Editorial Director; Marianne Hiland, Executive Editor; Richard Easby, Editorial Manager; Jim Hiscott, Design Manager; Kristin Hanneman, Illustrations Manager; Matt Wascavage, Manager of Publishing Services; Sean Philpotts, Production Manager.

EDITORIAL MANAGEMENT
Morrison BookWorks, LLC

PROGRAM CONSULTANTS
Dr. Shirley V. Dickson, Program Director, Literacy, Education Commission of the States; James A. Shymansky, E. Desmond Lee Professor of Science Education, University of Missouri-St. Louis.

National Geographic Theme Sets program developed by Macmillan Education Australia, Pty Limited.

Published by the National Geographic Society
1145 17th Street, N.W.
Washington, D.C. 20036-4688

ISBN: 978-0-7922-4741-8
ISBN: 0-7922-4741-8

Printed in Hong Kong.

2011 2010 2009 2008
4 5 6 7 8 9 10 11 12 13 14 15

Contents

Life Cycles

All animals go through different stages of growth between the time they are born and the time they die. These stages in an animal's life make up the animal's life cycle. Giant pandas, monarch butterflies, poison dart frogs, and Komodo dragons all have life cycles. But not all animals go through the stages of their life cycles in the same way.

 ## Key Concepts ....

1. The life cycle of animals moves through birth, growth, and reproduction, and ends at death.
2. The physical features of all animals change as they grow, but some animals change more than others.
3. Inherited behaviors are passed to offspring. Learned behaviors are taught.

Four Kinds of Life Cycles

Giant Pandas

Giant pandas are mammals that give birth to live babies.

Monarch Butterflies

Monarch butterflies are insects that hatch from eggs as caterpillars.

In this book you will learn about the life cycle of Komodo dragons.

Poison Dart Frogs

Poison dart frogs are amphibians that hatch from eggs as tadpoles.

Komodo Dragons

Komodo dragons are reptiles that hatch from eggs.

The Life Cycle of
Komodo Dragons

How would you feel if you came face to face with the flesh-eating Komodo dragon? Despite their name and fearful appearance, Komodo dragons are not really dragons. They are actually lizards, and they go through several stages of growth during their lifetime.

Komodo dragons are the world's largest lizards. They belong to a family of lizards called **monitors**. Monitor lizards have long necks, narrow heads, pointed snouts, powerful limbs, and muscular tails. They also have long forked tongues.

A Typical Reptile

Like all lizards, Komodo dragons are **reptiles**. Reptiles are egg-laying animals with a backbone and a tough skin covered with scales. They are **cold-blooded** and thus unable to regulate their own body heat. To get warm, they absorb heat directly from the sun, and they need shade to keep cool.

A Komodo dragon

Komodo dragons live on the islands of Komodo, Rinca, and Flores in Indonesia, a country in Asia. There is little rainfall there, and the summers can be very hot.

Komodo dragons warm their bodies by spending a few hours in the sun each day. If the day gets too warm, they stay cool in the shade or on a moist surface like the bank of a stream.

Today, there are only between 2,500 and 5,000 Komodo dragons left. They have disappeared from the Indonesian island of Padar, where they were once plentiful, because the deer that they used to eat have mostly disappeared. Komodos have also almost disappeared from the northwest coast of the island of Flores.

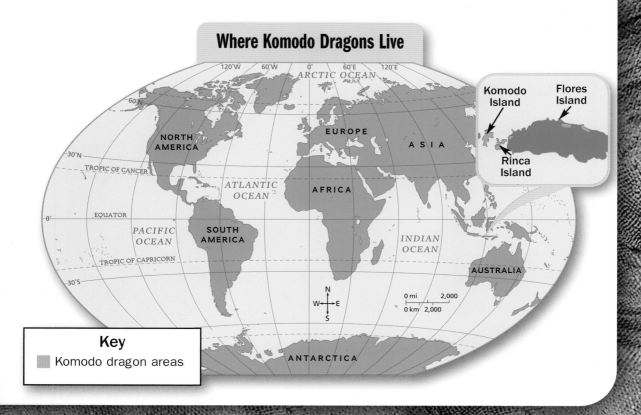

Where Komodo Dragons Live

Komodo Island
Flores Island
Rinca Island

ARCTIC OCEAN
NORTH AMERICA
EUROPE
ASIA
ATLANTIC OCEAN
AFRICA
PACIFIC OCEAN
SOUTH AMERICA
INDIAN OCEAN
AUSTRALIA
ANTARCTICA

TROPIC OF CANCER
EQUATOR
TROPIC OF CAPRICORN

120°W 60°W 0° 60°E 120°E
60°N
30°N
0°
30°S

0 mi   2,000
0 km   2,000

N
W   E
S

Key
Komodo dragon areas

Key Concept 1 The life cycle of animals moves through birth, growth, and reproduction, and ends at death.

Birth

As with all reptiles, the **life cycle** of a Komodo dragon begins when a female Komodo dragon lays her eggs. Female Komodos lay a **clutch** of about 20–40 soft, leathery eggs at a time. The eggs, about twice the size of chicken eggs, take eight to nine months to hatch.

life cycle
all the stages in
an animal's life

Komodo **hatchlings** are born with green bodies and yellow and black markings on their backs. As soon as they are born, Komodo hatchlings are capable of eating small birds and insects.

A Komodo dragon's egg

Growth

Komodo hatchlings measure about 30–40 centimeters (12–16 inches) and weigh about 100 grams (3.5 ounces) when they are born. They spend the first two or three years of their lives living in trees. This environment keeps them safe from larger Komodos, which often eat smaller Komodos. Living in trees also makes hunting easier for the young Komodos, since they do not have to compete with adult Komodos for food. In the trees, young Komodos feed on small birds, birds' eggs, and insects.

Within a year, Komodo dragons are more than double their birth size. They begin coming down from the trees in search of larger **prey**. However, it is not until they are about four years old and about 1.2 meters (4 feet) long that they start living on the ground all the time.

Komodo dragons continue to grow throughout their lives. The average weight of an adult Komodo is about 70 kilograms (154 pounds), and its typical length is about 2.7 meters (9 feet). The largest recorded Komodo dragon measured 3.13 meters (10.2 feet) long and weighed 165.9 kilograms (365.7 pounds).

A young Komodo dragon

Reproduction

The next stage of the Komodo dragon's life cycle is **reproduction**. Reproduction is the making of **offspring**, or babies. Komodo dragons, like most other reptiles, hatch from eggs.

reproduction
the making of
offspring, or babies

Reproduction begins with the joining of cells from two Komodo dragon parents. The cells from the female are called eggs. The cells from the male are called sperms. When eggs and sperms are joined, the eggs are **fertilized**, and offspring will begin to develop.

As with all reptiles, the eggs of the Komodo dragon are fertilized inside the body of the female. A leathery shell develops around each of the eggs. Then the female Komodo lays 20–40 eggs on land. Each egg provides a safe place for an **embryo**, or developing baby, until it is ready to hatch.

Komodo dragons are ready to reproduce when they are five to seven years old. Komodos are mostly **solitary** creatures, living by themselves. But males and females need to find each other in order to reproduce, or **breed**. They may meet when they come together to eat at the same food source.

Five to seven weeks after the eggs have been fertilized, the female Komodo lays her eggs. Usually she lays the eggs in burrows that she digs in a hillside or in warm, sandy ground. Sometimes she uses old birds' nests.

Lifespan

The lifespan of Komodo dragons in captivity is about 25 years, but in the wild they can live up to 50 years. When they are small, young Komodos are in danger of being killed by snakes, big birds of prey, and larger Komodos. But as adults, they have almost no natural **predators**.

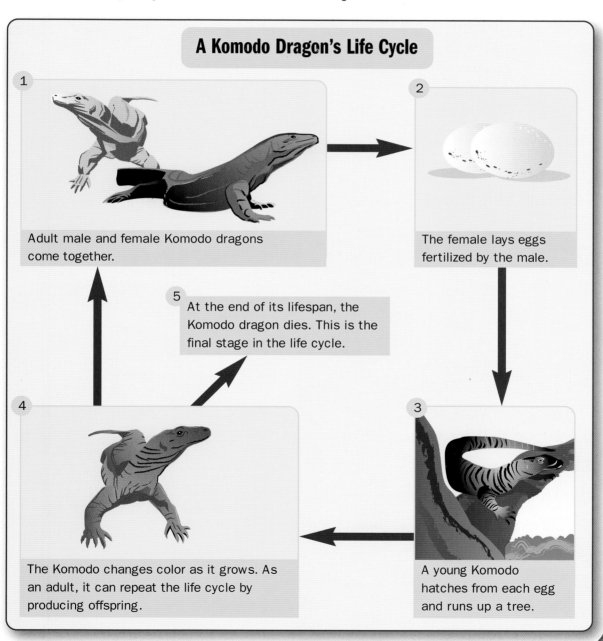

A Komodo Dragon's Life Cycle

1. Adult male and female Komodo dragons come together.

2. The female lays eggs fertilized by the male.

3. A young Komodo hatches from each egg and runs up a tree.

4. The Komodo changes color as it grows. As an adult, it can repeat the life cycle by producing offspring.

5. At the end of its lifespan, the Komodo dragon dies. This is the final stage in the life cycle.

Key Concept 2 The physical features of all animals change as they grow, but some animals change more than others.

From Egg to Komodo Dragon

Like many reptiles, young Komodo dragons develop inside an egg. The egg contains a food supply called a yolk for the embryo to use as it grows. By the time the young Komodos hatch, their **physical features** are very similar to those of adults. There are some differences between the adults and the young Komodos, however.

> physical features
> the parts of an animal's body that can be seen

Size and Color Komodo hatchlings are much smaller than adults, and the color of their skin is different from that of their parents. The yellow, black, and brick-red markings on the hatchlings' green bodies fade to reddish-brown patterns as the babies grow.

Tail The hatchlings' bodies are long and thin, and their tails are longer in proportion to their bodies than those of adults. The long tail and slim body make climbing and living in trees easy. As Komodos mature and start living on the ground, their tails grow large and thick. An adult Komodo can stand upright on the ground using its tail for support.

A Komodo hatches from an egg.

Legs Komodos are born with four short, stumpy legs. Their legs have strong muscles, and their feet have powerful claws. As the Komodos grow, their legs become stronger and more powerful. Adult Komodos use their strong legs to dig burrows and to chase their prey. Komodos attack the prey's feet first, knocking it off balance. Adult Komodos prey upon animals like deer, wild boar, and goats.

Jaws Komodos have powerful lower jaws that get stronger as they grow. Their jaws can open very wide, allowing them to swallow large chunks of meat. Komodos' stomachs expand easily, so the animals are able to consume huge quantities of food. In fact, adult Komodos can eat up to 80 percent of their body weight in one sitting. It takes a Komodo several days to digest a big meal, so it can survive for days without eating again.

Teeth Komodos grow new teeth all through the growth and reproduction stages. These sharp teeth are very useful for tearing meat, but not for chewing. Komodos do not chew their food; they swallow it in large pieces. Often they break their teeth while eating, but new teeth quickly grow in. Komodo dragons can grow up to 200 new teeth every year.

A Komodo dragon uses its forked tongue to pick up the scent of its prey.

Key Concept 3 Inherited behaviors are passed to offspring. Learned behaviors are taught.

Komodo Dragon Behaviors

All animals have a set of behaviors that makes them act in a certain way. A female Komodo dragon uses instinct to find a safe place to lay her eggs. This is an inherited behavior. **Inherited behaviors** are qualities that are passed down from **generation** to generation. They are automatic; individuals do not have to learn them.

> *inherited behaviors*
> ways of acting that animals are born with

Inherited behaviors are different from **learned behaviors**. Learned behaviors are taught to the offspring by an adult or learned by the animal during its lifetime. Young Komodo dragons are on their own from the day they are born, so they do not learn any behaviors from their parents. Their behaviors are the result of inherited behaviors.

> *learned behaviors*
> ways of acting that animals learn during their lifetime

Komodo dragons are mostly solitary creatures, so they do not learn any behaviors.

Finding Shelter Komodo dragons have several inherited behaviors that help them find shelter and survive. Young Komodo dragons are at risk of being eaten by older Komodo dragons. As soon as a Komodo dragon is born, it will run up a tree. It knows instinctively that the tree will shelter it from bigger Komodos. The tree will also provide it with a food source. In the trees, young Komodos feed on small insects, birds, and birds' eggs. They do not need to venture down from the trees to find food.

Inherited behaviors also help Komodo dragons survive the heat and cold. Komodos know how and where to dig burrows in which to take shelter from the weather. The burrows are usually dug on open hillsides or dry creek beds. Komodos use their strong feet to dig burrows up to 9 meters (29.5 feet) long.

Female Komodo dragons know to lay their eggs in holes dug on hill slopes or in the nests of large birds to keep the eggs warm and shelter them from predators.

A Komodo dragon shelters in a burrow it has dug for protection.

Feeding Behaviors Mature Komodo dragons show inherited behaviors when they are hunting and feeding. Komodos eat almost every part of their prey, including bones, fur, hides, and hooves. However, Komodos instinctively know to avoid eating a prey animal's waste products. Young Komodo dragons, in danger from older Komodos, sometimes roll in animal waste. They know that the older Komodos will avoid this smell. This is also an inherited behavior.

When hunting, Komodo dragons sometimes show another inherited behavior. They can tell when a female prey animal is pregnant by her smell. They keep track of pregnant female animals because after the female gives birth, her newborn makes an easy meal.

Komodo dragons are also born with an excellent swimming ability, which helps them in their search for prey. They swim by moving their tails from side to side while keeping their legs by their sides. Komodos will swim from one island to another if it offers a better supply of food.

Komodos are excellent swimmers.

Think About the Key Concepts

Think about what you read. Think about the pictures and diagrams. Use these to answer the questions. Share what you think with others.

1. What are the four basic stages in every animal's life cycle?

2. For animals to reproduce, what type of cell is needed from the male parent and the female parent?

3. What are some changes that happen to animals as they grow?

4. What makes inherited behaviors different from learned behaviors?

Flow Diagram

Diagrams use pictures and words to explain ideas.
You can learn new ideas without having to read many words.

There are different kinds of diagrams.
The diagram on page 19 is a **flow diagram**. A flow diagram uses pictures and words to explain the different stages in a process. Some flow diagrams circle around to show that a process repeats itself. Look back at the diagram on page 11. It is a flow diagram that shows a Komodo dragon's life cycle.

How to Read a Flow Diagram

1. Read the title.
The title tells you what the diagram is about.

2. Study the pictures.
The pictures illustrate the different stages in the process.

3. Read the captions.
The captions explain what happens at each stage.

4. Follow the numbers and arrows.
The numbers show the order of the stages. The arrows help show the direction of the flow diagram.

How a Komodo Gets Its Food

1 The Komodo eats dead prey.

2 Meat trapped in the Komodo's teeth breeds bacteria.

5 If the prey escapes, bacteria from the Komodo's bite usually kill the prey.

3 The Komodo's forked tongue senses live prey.

4 The Komodo chases and attacks the prey.

Read the Diagram

Read the diagram by following the steps on page 18. Write down what you learned. Discuss the different stages with a classmate. Describe to your classmate what you learned from the diagram.

News Report

A **news report** gives information about current events or topics in the news. You may read news reports in newspapers or in news magazines. The report starting on page 21 tells you about a Komodo-dragon exhibit.

A news report includes the following:

Tacoma, April 14

The **date** tells when the article was written.

Deadly Dragon on Display

The **headline** tells what the report is about.

The **lead** gives the important facts in a sentence or two.

From tomorrow until early October, the Point Defiance Zoo in Tacoma, Washington, will host Loki, a 2.3-meter (7.5-foot) long Indonesian Komodo dragon, the first of its kind to visit the Pacific Northwest. Loki will be the star of an exhibit called "The Dragon's Lair."

Loki, the Komodo dragon at Point Defiance Zoo

Photographs, maps, or diagrams support the text.

The Headline
The headline summarizes the content of the report in just a few words and makes the reader want to read on.

The Lead
The lead gives the reader the most important information in a single sentence or short paragraph.

The Body Paragraphs
The body paragraphs develop the report. They may provide background information. They often contain quotations from people who know about the topic.

Deadly Dragon on Display

Tacoma, April 14

The **date** tells when the article was written.

The **headline** tells what the report is about.

The **lead** gives the important facts in a sentence or two.

From tomorrow until early October, the Point Defiance Zoo in Tacoma, Washington, will host Loki, a 2.3-meter (7.5-foot) long Indonesian Komodo dragon, the first of its kind to visit the Pacific Northwest. Loki will be the star of an exhibit called "The Dragon's Lair."

Loki, the Komodo dragon at Point Defiance Zoo

Photographs, maps, or diagrams support the text.

Loki, who is used to Indonesia's hot climate, is being kept in a special climate-controlled cage. He weighs 34 kilograms (75 pounds), has scales the color of bark, and possesses a long forked tongue that slides out from between his fangs. Like other Komodo dragons, Loki can attack and kill animals as big as water buffalo.

Besides eating other animals, Komodo dragons are also cannibalistic. Male Komodo dragons have even been known to eat their own offspring. Komodos also occasionally eat humans, so it is no surprise that Komodos have a reputation for being fierce.

However, despite the dragon's name, visitors expecting to see a giant, fire-breathing creature will be disappointed. Komodos are actually lizards, not dragons.

Komodo dragons are lizards, not the fire-breathing creatures of myths.

"Komodo dragons have been very popular at other zoos where they've been hosted, and I believe it has to do with people's fascination with the idea of dragons," says Point Defiance marketing manager Sally Perkins. "There have been many rumors about the Komodo dragon and its size. We want people to come and see Loki so they can understand this animal for what it really is."

According to veterinarian Dr. Holly Reed, some people believe that when the Chinese first sailed to Indonesia, they came across the Komodo and were so impressed by the size of the lizard that they went home with stories of a giant dragon they had discovered. The purpose of the Point Defiance exhibit is to familiarize people with a real Komodo dragon.

Quotations give information from someone who knows about the topic.

Point Defiance Zoo in Tacoma, where Loki is on display

 **Komodo Dragon Facts**

- The scientific name for Komodo dragon is *Varanus komodoensis*.

- The Komodo dragon is the biggest living lizard in the world.

- There are four times as many male Komodo dragons as there are females in the wild.

- A Komodo dragon can run faster than 24 kilometers (15 miles) per hour.

- The saliva of a Komodo dragon contains four kinds of bacteria. There are no known medicines that will kill the bacteria.

Komodo Dragons in the Wild

Subheads can introduce background information.

In the wild, Komodos can be found only on a few islands in Indonesia. Komodo Island is their largest single habitat. About 2,500–5,000 Komodo dragons live there.

Fossil remains of creatures similar to Komodo dragons have provided scientists with some clues about Komodos' ancestors. These fossils date back to the Jurassic period nearly 130 million years ago.

The fossils suggest that Komodos became extinct everywhere on Earth except on these islands. The islands' isolation played a role in helping Komodos survive.

The islands also provide Komodos with a suitable habitat—a hot, dry climate with grasslands and forest clearings. Komodos prefer to make their burrows behind overhanging vegetation, rocks, or tree roots.

Komodo Dragon Habitats

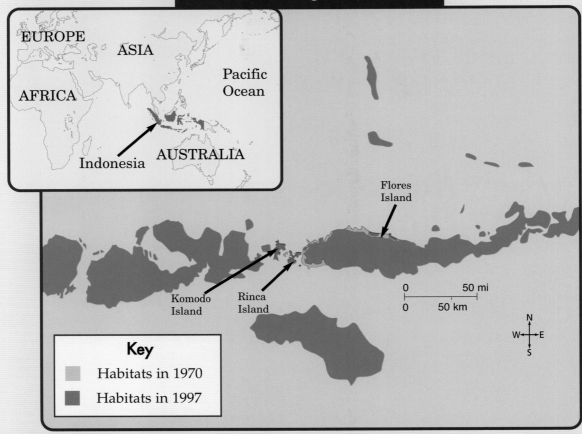

EUROPE
ASIA
Pacific Ocean
AFRICA
Indonesia
AUSTRALIA

Flores Island
Komodo Island
Rinca Island

0   50 mi
0   50 km

N
W E
S

Key
- Habitats in 1970
- Habitats in 1997

Komodo Dragons in Zoos

Zoos in many parts of the world have introduced special programs called captive-breeding programs to try to save the Komodo dragon. These programs, which allow Komodos to be bred in zoos, have been very successful. Today, there are about 100 Komodos that have been bred in zoos across the world.

"The prime function of zoos is conservation," says Point Defiance Zoo's deputy director John Houck.

"Conservation continues to be an issue worldwide. Exhibits like this allow us to talk about endangered species. We're trying to motivate people to make wise decisions in the natural world."

The Komodo's main food sources are deer, boars, goats, pigs, and, in Loki's case, frozen rats. Loki can eat food equal to 80 percent of his body weight in one sitting.

"Loki is ... giving our staff a great chance to learn about caring for such a unique and dangerous creature," says Dr. Brian Joseph, chief veterinarian and general curator at Point Defiance Zoo.

This Komodo dragon in Honolulu Zoo was from the first group hatched by the breeding program at the National Zoo in Washington, D.C.

Joining Loki at the exhibit will be other Southeast Asian animals—Java rice sparrows, crested wood partridges, a carpet python, Tokay geckos, and a desert sand goanna. "Our goal is to bring people together with animals so that they go home and say, 'I've seen that animal.' That may give them reason enough to care," says Perkins.

While Loki is on loan, his adult sister, Raptura, and a juvenile female will become permanent residents of Seattle's Woodland Park Zoo next month. The Woodland Park exhibit will provide the Komodo dragons with the right kind of environment. They will have a hot and dry forest, a small pool for cooling, heated rocks, natural and artificial sunlight for basking, and soil for digging.

The exhibit opens May 27. Loki will continue to star at Point Defiance Zoo throughout the summer.

People observe Komodo dragons at a zoo.

Apply the Key Concepts

Key Concept 1 The life cycle of animals moves through birth, growth, and reproduction, and ends at death.

Activity

Choose one stage of the Komodo dragon's life cycle. Draw and label a picture of a Komodo dragon during this stage. Then write a brief description of what happens to a Komodo dragon during this stage.

Komodo Dragon Hatchling

Key Concept 2 The physical features of all animals change as they grow, but some animals change more than others.

Activity

Draw a Venn diagram to show in which ways Komodo hatchlings look the same as and different from their parents. Label one circle "Komodo Hatchlings" and the other circle "Adult Komodos."

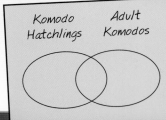

Komodo Hatchlings   Adult Komodos

Key Concept 3 Inherited behaviors are passed to offspring. Learned behaviors are taught.

Activity

Use what you have learned about the Komodo dragon to make a list of its behaviors. List at least three behaviors and label each one "inherited behavior" or "learned behavior."

Komodo Dragon Behaviors

_____

_____

_____

Write Your Own News Report

You have read the news report about Komodo dragons. Now it is time to write your own news report about an animal.

1. Study the Model

Look back at the news report on pages 21–26. Find the important features of news reports. Think about how the headline summarizes the report and makes it sound interesting. Think about the information contained in the first paragraph. Read the body text again. Notice the detailed information. Notice the quotations from various people who know about the topic.

Writing a News Report

◆ Choose a current event or topic in the news.

◆ Use a headline that grabs readers' attention.

◆ Write the most important information in the lead.

◆ Include quotations from people who know about the topic.

2. Choose Your Topic

Now think about a topic you can write your report about. The report should be about a current event or topic in the news, and it should have to do with an animal. You may choose to write about an endangered animal. You may choose to write about a special event at your local zoo. Or you may choose to write about another topic related to animals. Read the newspapers and search the Internet for ideas for a topic. Look for a topic that includes quotations from people with information or opinions.

3. Research Your Topic

Write down a list of questions that you will answer in your article. Think of *who, what, when, where, why,* and *how* questions. Research your topic to answer your questions. Take notes on important information. Write down any interesting quotes you find. Look for pictures and diagrams to include in your report.

Topic: Endangered Toad

1. In which country is the toad found?

2. Why has the toad become endangered?

4. Write a Draft

Put your notes in an order that makes sense. Then write a draft of your report. Remember to put the most important information in the first paragraph, using a sentence or two. Add more detailed information in the body text. Include quotes.

5. Revise and Edit

Read over your draft. Make corrections as you go. Double check any dates, times, or other facts against your research. Make sure any names are spelled correctly.

When you are happy with your article, write a headline. Make sure it summarizes your report in a few words and makes people want to keep reading.

Create a Magazine of News Reports

Now you can get together with the rest of the class to create a magazine of news reports.

How to Make a News Magazine

1. **Look at a news magazine.**
   Read the contents page and find the articles. Look at how the articles are arranged on the pages.

2. **Type your article.**
   Type your news report into two columns and print it out.

3. **Find a photograph to go with your article.**
   Print a photograph or two from the Internet, or photocopy one from a newspaper or news magazine. The photograph should show what your article is about. Paste the photograph under your report.

4. **Write a caption for your photograph.**
   The caption will say what is happening in the photograph. The caption should relate to the report.

5. **Put the news magazine together.**
   Put all the class news reports together. Number the pages.

6. **Create a contents page.**
   Write a list of the names of the news reports in the order they appear in the magazine. Write the page number next to the name of each report.

7. **Create a cover.**
   Choose a name for your news magazine and write it on the cover. Choose a good photograph from one of the news reports that you can copy and paste on the cover.